# Recorder from the Beginning Book 3

## John Pitts

This recorder course in 3 stages has been designed for children aged 7 upwards. Since publication it has become one of the most popular schemes used in many parts of the world. **Recorder from the Beginning** assumes no previous knowledge of either music or the recorder, and full explanations are provided at every stage so that specialist teaching is not essential. Teacher's Books are available for each stage, and these contain simple piano accompaniments, guitar chord symbols and suggestions for each tune.

Cassette tapes of accompaniments are now available, in response to popular demand. These include a model version of each tune, followed by exciting rhythmic accompaniments for recorders to play along with, both in school and at home.

The new coloured edition of the books has allowed more emphasis on activities directly related to aspects of Music in the National Curriculum. For example, opportunities are provided for recorder players to be accompanied by instrumental ostinati and other percussion accompaniments and for recorders to perform with singers in two-part items, rounds, songs with descants and other activities.

John Pitts 1993

**Acknowledgements**

The publishers would like to thank the following for permission to include their copyright material: Spike Milligan *On the Ning Nang Nong* from *Silly Verse for Kids* by Spike Milligan published by Dobson Books; *Paddy McGinty's Goat* © 1917 Francis, Day and Hunter reproduced by permission of EMI Music Publishing Ltd; *O Little Town of Bethlehem* Tune: Arranged by R. Vaughan Williams from the *English Hymnal* by permission of Oxford University Press, Descant: by Thomas Armstrong, © The Royal School of Church Music, and reprinted by permission. The music on the following pages has been specially composed and arranged for this book by the author: 2, 11 12, 18, 20, 28 (top), 30 (top), 35, 37, 38, 40, 41, 45, 46 (bottom), 47 (top).

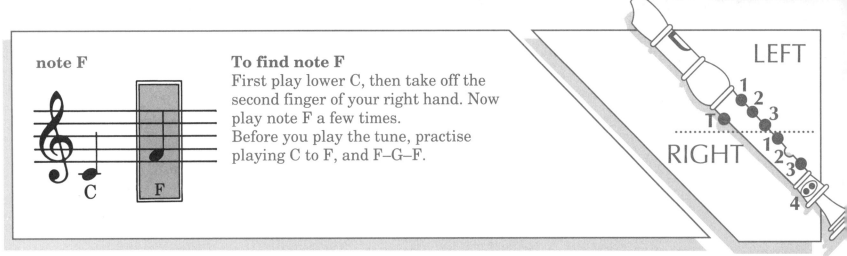

**note F**

**To find note F**
First play lower C, then take off the
second finger of your right hand. Now
play note F a few times.
Before you play the tune, practise
playing C to F, and F–G–F.

## On the Ning Nang Nong

On the Ning Nang Nong Where the cows go Bong! And the Mon-keys all say Boo!

There's a Nong Nang Ning Where the trees go Ping! And the tea pots Jibber Jabber Joo.

On the Nong Ning Nang All the mice go Clang! And you just can't catch 'em when they do!

So it's Ning Nang Nong! Cows go Bong! Nong Ning Nang! The mice go Clang! What a
Nong Nang Ning! Trees go Ping!

noi — sy place to be-long _____ , Is the Ning Nang Ning Nang Nong!

More tunes using note F

## Apusski du

## Little Brown Jug   An optional second part has stems down.

Chorus

# Debka Hora (Israeli dance)

# Old Texas

All learn Recorder 1 part first. Then split into two groups.
Recorder 2 is the same tune but begins one bar later.
When this happens we call the tune a CANON.
Later, ask some friends to sing the song while you play Recorder 2.

Recorder 1 (or voice)

I'm going to    leave _____ old Tex-as    now _____, They've got no

Recorder 2

I'm going to leave _____ old    Tex-as    now _____,

use _____ for the long-horn cow _____.

They've got    no    use _____ for the long-horn    cow _____.

4

# Time Signatures

So far we have used time signatures like these:

The TOP NUMBER tells us HOW MANY conductor's beats there are in each bar.
The NOTE UNDERNEATH shows us HOW MUCH each beat is worth.
Now we must use proper time signatures, with numbers at the bottom instead of notes.

The BOTTOM NUMBER tells us HOW MUCH each beat is worth.
Remember we are counting the conductor's BEATS, not the notes.
We can have any number of notes in a bar.
But they must add up to the same value as the conductor's beats.
Here are some examples.
Each of them has 3 conductor's beats in each bar.

$\frac{3}{2}$ means that there will be three Half Note ($\frac{1}{2}$ note) beats in each bar.
The notes in each bar add up to the same value as the conductor's beats.

$\frac{3}{4}$ means that there will be three Quarter Note ($\frac{1}{4}$ note) beats in each bar.
The notes add up to the same value.

$\frac{3}{8}$ means that there will be three Eighth Note ($\frac{1}{8}$ note) beats in each bar.
The notes add up to the same value.

5

In the next tune, the **3/4** Time Signature means that there will be three Quarter note ($\frac{1}{4}$ note) beats in each bar. (The notes add up to the same value.)

## Santa Lucia

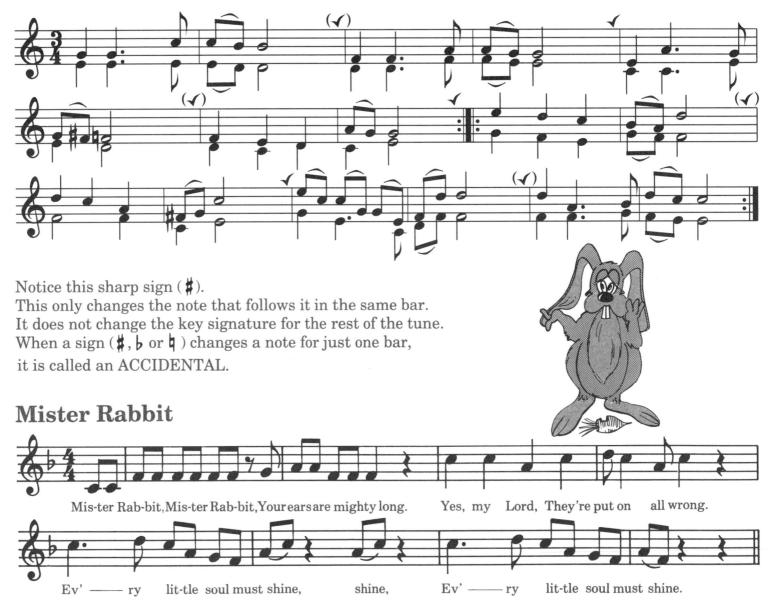

Notice this sharp sign (♯).
This only changes the note that follows it in the same bar.
It does not change the key signature for the rest of the tune.
When a sign (♯, ♭ or ♮) changes a note for just one bar,
it is called an ACCIDENTAL.

## Mister Rabbit

Mis-ter Rab-bit, Mis-ter Rab-bit, Your ears are mighty long.     Yes, my    Lord,  They're put on    all wrong.

Ev' —— ry    lit-tle soul must shine,         shine,         Ev' —— ry    lit-tle soul must shine.

# There's a Tavern in the Town

For a duet and extra tunes using notes and rhythms met so far, see 'Recorder from the Beginning' Tune Book 3, pages 4 to 7.

## Class Activity

When you know the next tune, try it as a round. **Singers** (or recorders) can be Group 1, with Recorders as Group 2. You can use the phrase marked A as an **ostinato** to play on xylophone. Let the ostinato begin first.

## Canadian Canoe Song (Two–part round)

My paddle's keen and bright, Flash-ing with sil-ver,

Fol-low the wild goose flight, Dip, dip and swing.

note B♭ (B flat)

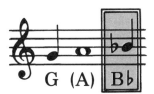

G (A) B♭

**To find note B♭ (B flat)**
First play note G, then raise your left middle finger. At the same time add on your right hand first finger. Now play note B♭. Before you play the tune practise the first bar slowly.

**Remember**
The B♭ in the Key Signature at the beginning of the stave turns each B into B♭.
This saves writing a flat sign before each B.

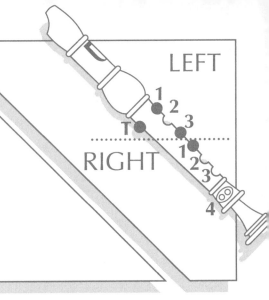

LEFT

RIGHT

## Zum Gali Gali   All learn Recorder 1 part first. Then split into two groups.

(1 and 2)

1

2

## Go down Moses

When Is-rael was in E-gypt's land, Let my people go.

Op-pressed so hard they could not stand, Let my peo-ple go.

Go down, Mo-ses, Way down in E-gypt's land,

Tell ole Pha-roah, Let my peo-ple go.

## Coventry Carol (English, 15th century)

# Two Shanties

Notice the natural sign (♮) in bar 1 of 'Boney'.
This is an accidental (see page 6).

## Boney was a Warrior (Halliards Shanty)

Bo-ney was a war — ri - or, Way — ay — yah!

Bo - ney went to Wa - ter-loo, Way — ay — yah!

## Fire Down Below (Capstan Shanty)

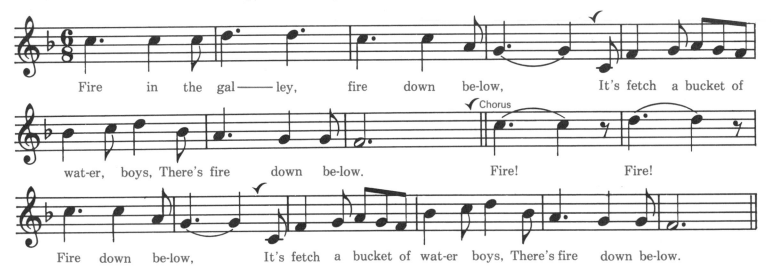

Fire in the gal — ley, fire down be-low, It's fetch a bucket of

wat-er, boys, There's fire down be-low. Fire! Fire!

Fire down be-low, It's fetch a bucket of wat-er boys, There's fire down be-low.

## Playing the tied notes

First play this:
Take care with the slur
Accent the G marked >.

Now join (tie) both G
notes together.

When you can play the tune, ask a friend to accompany you.
They can use piano, guitar, or chime bars.
All the music is in the Teacher's Book.
Or you can use the cassette accompaniment tape.

## Crombie's Boogie © JCP

## Cudelia Brown (Jamaican Folksong)

All learn Recorder 1 part first. Then split into two groups.
Later, ask some friends to sing the song while you play Recorder 2.
There are two rhythm **ostinati** in the Teacher's Book.

For another duet and a round see 'Recorder from the Beginning' Tune Book 3, pages 8 and 9.

Arrangement © JCP

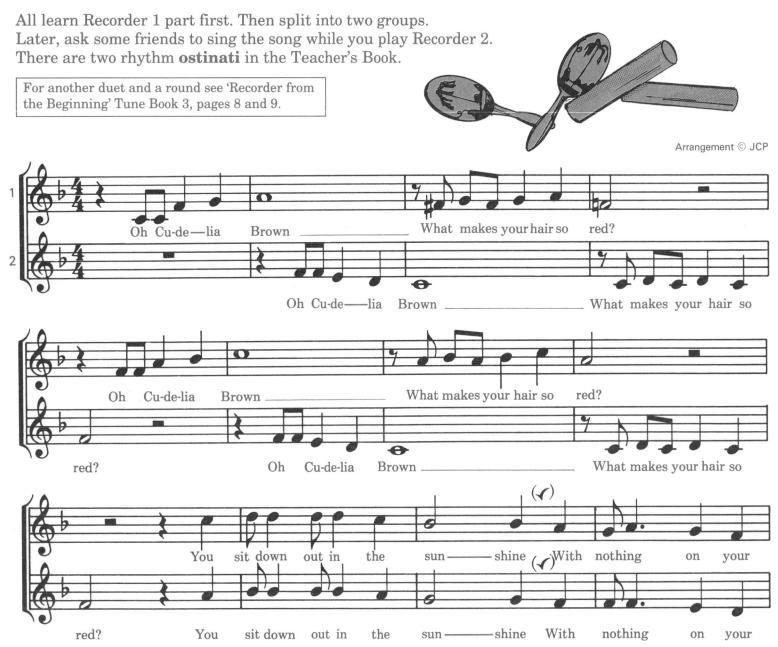

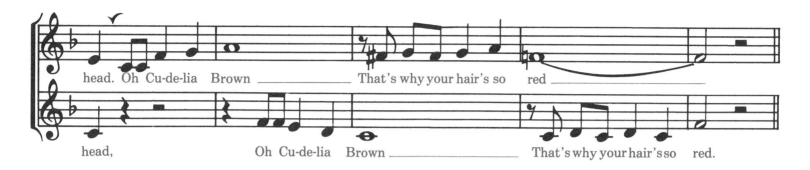

head. Oh Cu-de-lia Brown _____ That's why your hair's so red _____

head,       Oh Cu-de-lia Brown _____ That's why your hair's so red.

## La Cucaracha   (Mexican dance)

## Cossack Love Song

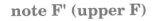

**note F' (upper F)**

F    F'

**To find note F' (upper F)**
First play lower F.
Then pinch your left thumb, to uncover about one third of the hole (as for upper E).
At the same time take off your right hand fourth finger.
Tongue firmly.
Use slightly stronger breath for upper F than lower F.

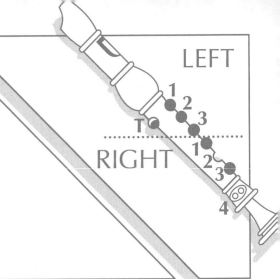

For three duets and other tunes using note F' see 'Recorder from the Beginning' Tune Book 3, pages 10 to 15.

## The Swazi Warrior

## Auld Lang Syne

## Another tune with accompaniment

The tune has note stems up.
The accompaniment has note stems down.

## Ade, zur guten Nacht  (Farewell, goodnight)

# Waltzing Matilda (Australian)

Chorus

# Star of County Down (Irish)

# Tambourin (French dance, 18th century)

Rameau

# Why shouldn't my goose? (Four-part round)

Class Activity For suggestions see page 7.

Why should-n't my goose Grow so fat as thy goose, When I paid for my goose Twice as much as thine?

# Ho there, Punchinello (Three-part round)

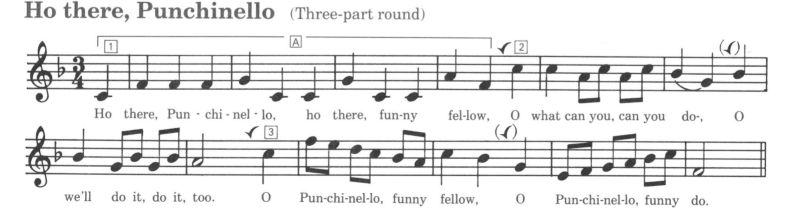

Ho there, Pun-chi-nel-lo, ho there, fun-ny fel-low, O what can you, can you do-, O

we'll do it, do it, too. O Pun-chi-nel-lo, funny fellow, O Pun-chi-nel-lo, funny do.

note F#' (upper F sharp)

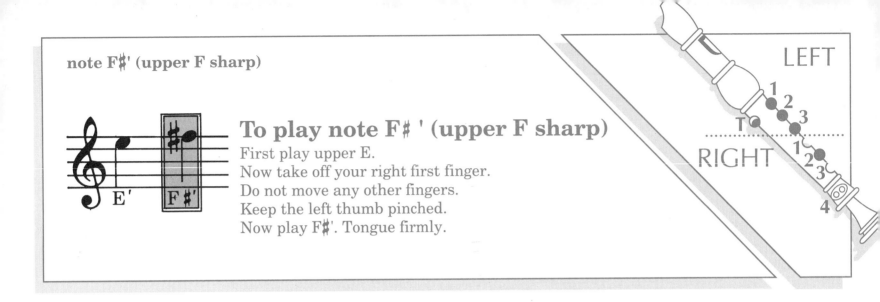

**To play note F# ' (upper F sharp)**
First play upper E.
Now take off your right first finger.
Do not move any other fingers.
Keep the left thumb pinched.
Now play F#'. Tongue firmly.

## Polka for Paula

© JCP

For a duet and other tunes using note F♯ see 'Recorder from the Beginning' Tune Book 3, pages 18 and 19.

## March from 'Scipio' (Handel)

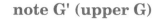

**note G' (upper G)**

E'  F'  G'

## To play note G' (upper G)

The fingering is the same as for lower G
except that the left thumb is pinched.

Start on upper E and move upwards step by step.
Play E' — F' — G', as written alongside here.

The Tango begins with notes E' — F' — G'.
It also uses note F♯'.
Practise the first two bars.
Then play the tune.

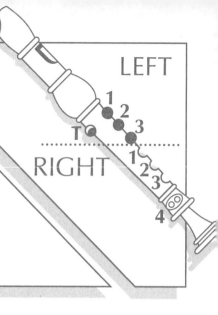

LEFT

RIGHT

## Tierra Tango

© JCP

Fine

D.C.

## Paddy McGinty's Goat

## St Patrick's Day (Irish Jig)

## March, 'See the conqu'ring hero' (Handel)

## Since first I saw your face (Elizabethan Song by Thomas Ford)

In the next tune you often get a quaver (eighth note) followed by a quaver rest 𝅘𝅥𝅮 𝄾
This sounds similar to a staccato crotchet (quarter note) 𝅘𝅥 so use 'tut' for tonguing.

Take care to play the legato (smooth) phrases in contrast.

## Soldiers' March (Schumann)

## The Wee Cooper o'Fife (Scotland)

This waltz is arranged as a Trio, for three players or groups of players.

The melody is in the 1st recorder part all the time. The other two parts are accompaniment only.

You can use other instruments instead of recorders for the accompaniment if you wish. These could be chime bars, glockenspiel, flutes or violins.

## German Waltz (Franz Schubert)

For a duet and other tunes using note G' see 'Recorder from the Beginning' Tune Book 3, pages 16 and 17.

## Andante Graziosa (Mozart)

note G♯ (G sharp)

## To find note G♯ (G sharp)

Play note A. Keep your fingers in position.
Now add on your right hand, first and
second fingers.
Look at this diagram to help you.

This is the fingering for note G♯.
Play it.

LEFT

RIGHT

Each part may finish in turn as usual.
Or you can finish together by stopping
on the notes marked 𝄐

## Miaou  (Three-part round)

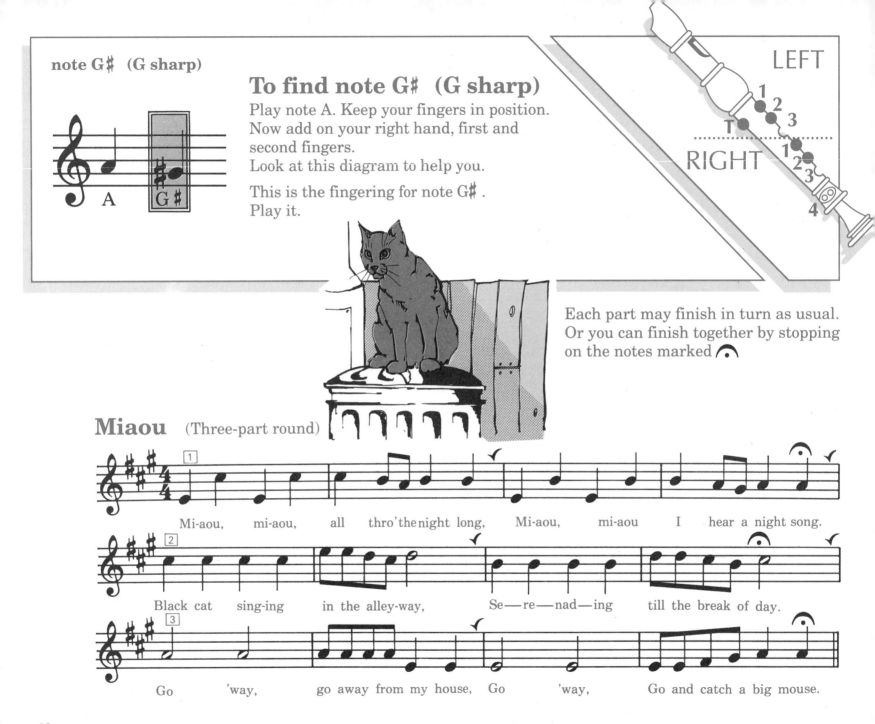

Mi-aou,  mi-aou,  all  thro'the night long,  Mi-aou,  mi-aou  I  hear a night song.

Black cat  sing-ing  in the alley-way,  Se—re—nad—ing  till the break of day.

Go  'way,  go away from my house,  Go  'way,  Go and catch a big mouse.

# Black Eyes (Russian Gypsy Song)

For three duets and other tunes see 'Recorder from the Beginning' Tune Book 3, pages 20 to 25.

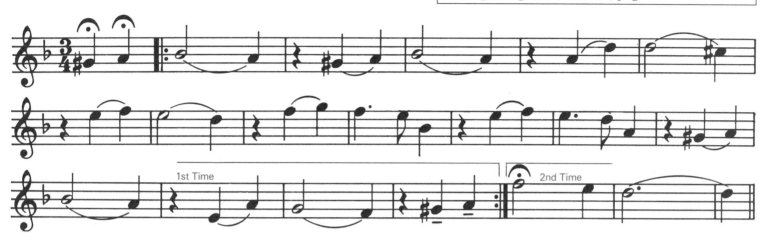

# Cavalry Patrol (Song of the Steppes)

Russian song by Knipper

## Mazurka Vistula

## Hava Nagila (Israel)

## Carols to play
### Away in a Manger (W.J. Kirkpatrick)

### Silent Night (F. Grüber)

(Includes F')

## Patapan (French) Arrangement © JCP

(Includes G♯)

## Deck the hall (Welsh)

(Includes F♯ ' and G')

## O Little Town of Bethlehem (Descant by T. Armstrong) *For note upper E♮, see page 32.*

## To play note E♭' (upper E♭)

Play upper D.
Keep your fingers in position.
Now add on your third left finger and the first three fingers of your right hand.

This leaves the top and bottom holes uncovered at the front, also the back thumb-hole uncovered.
Use the diagram to help you.

This is the fingering for E♭'. Play it.

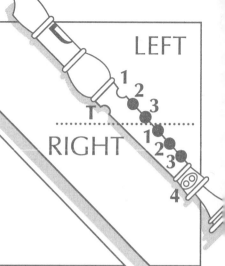

## Macaroni Tarantella

## Minuet in G minor (J. S. Bach)

For a duet with occasional use of E♭' see 'Recorder from the Beginning' Tune Book 3, page 28.

# New names for familiar fingerings (Enharmonic changes)

Some of the notes you have learnt have other names.
These are notes that have been changed by using a sharp ( $\sharp$ ) or flat ( $\flat$ ).

On the piano there are black notes in-between most of the white notes.
The black notes are the sharps and flats.
Look below at the diagram of part of a piano keyboard.

Find note upper E (E' ) and then note upper E$\flat$ (E$\flat$ '), the black note just below E' (to the left).
Now find note upper D (D') and then upper D$\sharp$ (D$\sharp$ '), the black note just above D' (to the right).

Notice that note E$\flat$' and note D$\sharp$' both use the same key on the piano.
All the other black notes also have two names for the same note.
See how note A$\flat$ is the same note as G$\sharp$ .
See how note C$\sharp$' (upper C$\sharp$ ) is the same note as D$\flat$ ' (upper D$\flat$ ).

Recorder notes work the same way, with two names for the same note.
We use the SAME FINGERING for both notes.
On the next page we learn a new name for a note we can play already.

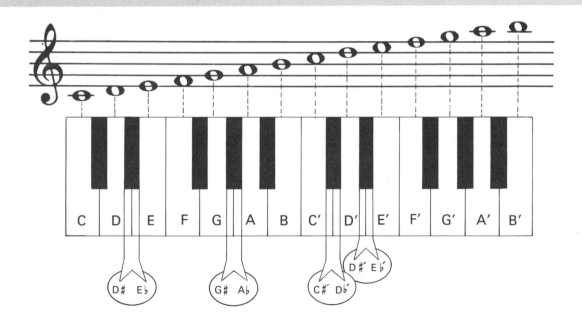

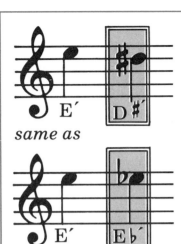

## To play note D#' (upper D# )

Play note upper E (E').

Now take off your left thumb and first finger. At the same time add on your right third finger.

Look at the diagram to help you.

This is the fingering for note D#'. Play it.

This note has the same fingering as upper E♭ (E♭'). Play both pairs of notes written alongside here.

*same as*

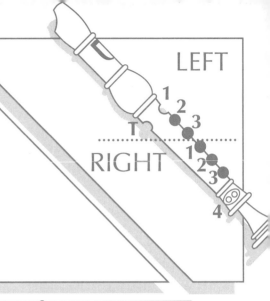

LEFT

RIGHT

For a duet see 'Recorder from the Beginning' Tune Book 3, page 30.

## Moscow Nights

# Homage to Schubert

## Alternative fingering

Some notes can be fingered in more than one way.
The alternative methods are often useful to play certain slurred notes more smoothly.
In the above tune, notes B to C' and B to D' are slurred.

Both these pairs of notes can be played more smoothly if, instead of using the left thumb and 1st
finger for note B, you use the left thumb together with the 2nd and 3rd fingers.
The places for using the alternative fingering are marked 2.
Usually you must decide for yourself when to use alternative fingering.

*For more details, see 'Advanced Recorder Technique' by Carl Dolmetsch, published by Thomas Nelson & Sons Ltd.*

## note E♭ (lower E flat)
## note D♯ (lower D sharp)

D

E♭

E

D♯

# Two new notes at once

Lower E flat and Lower D sharp.

We learnt two notes with the same fingering – upper E flat (E♭') and upper D sharp (D♯').
Next we learn lower E flat (E♭) and lower D sharp (D♯).
Both use the same fingering.

Play note D. Now slide the right hand third finger a little to the right.
This uncovers one of the small holes.
Look at the diagram to help you.
This is the fingering for E♭. Play it.

Now play note E (natural).
Add on your right third finger carefully.
Make sure it only covers the first small hole.

This is the fingering for D♯. Play it.

LEFT

1
2
3
T

RIGHT

1
2
3

4

## John Brown's Body (American)

This tune uses notes B♭ and E♭.

Chorus

The next tune uses note D♯.
What other sharps are in the Key Signature?
This tune is in the key of E major.

## Them Chiming Bells (Spiritual)

Arrangement © JCP

Ma-ry and Mar-tha just gone 'long, Ma-ry and Mar-tha just gone 'long.
Preacher and el-der Preacher and el-der

Ma-ry and Mar-tha just gone 'long to ring them chim-ing bells. Cry-ing
Preacher and el-der

Chorus

1 Free grace and dy-ing love, Free grace and dy-ing love,

2

Free grace and dy-ing love to ring them chim-ing bells.

Another tune in E major.
Take care to play all the sharps!
These are F♯, C♯, G♯ and D♯.

## Hold out your Light (Spiritual)

Hold out your light, you Heav'n bound sol-dier, Hold out your light, you Heav'n bound sol-dier,

Hold out your light, you Heav'n bound soldier, Let your light shine a-round the world.

Verse

O, dea-con can't you hold out your light? O, dea-con can't you hold out your light?
preacher preacher

O, dea-con can't you hold out your light? Let your light shine a-round the world.
preacher

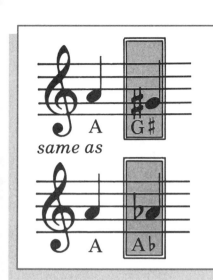

## Another name for a note we know already

Play note G♯.
Now look at the piano keyboard on page 33. We can see that G♯ is the same note as A♭.
On the recorder we use the same fingering for both notes.

Play note A.
Now play note A♭.

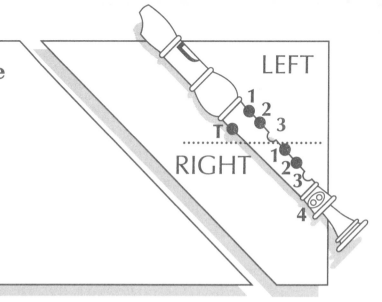

## This Train (Spiritual)

This train is bound for glory, this train;     This train is bound for glory, this train;

This train is bound for glory, I'm not telling you a story. This train is leaving, get on board!

## The New-born Child (from 'Cantata 122' by J. S. Bach)

## Two high notes:

A' (upper A) and G♯' (upper G sharp).

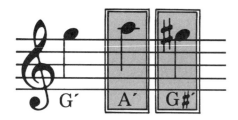

G'    A'    G♯'

For these high notes, keep the thumb-hole opening very small ⚫

First play upper G.
Now play upper A. This uses the same fingers as lower A except for the 'pinched' left thumb.

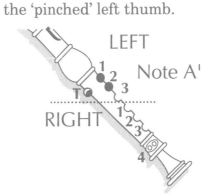

LEFT

Note A'

RIGHT

Play upper A.
Now add on your right first finger. This makes note G♯'. Play it.

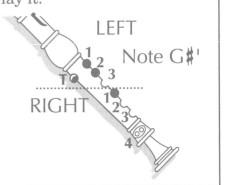

LEFT

Note G♯'

RIGHT

## Orljak Tango *(pronounce 'j' as 'y')*

© JCP

Fine

D.C.

40

For two duets that include note A' see 'Recorder from the Beginning' Tune Book 3, pages 26 and 27.

## Mattachins (French)

Arrangement © JCP

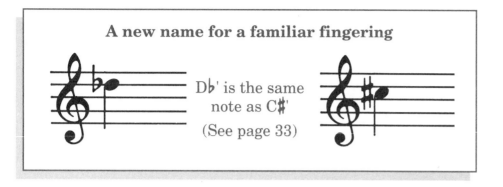

**A new name for a familiar fingering**

Db' is the same note as C#'

(See page 33)

Both tunes below use the same key signature of four flats: Bb, Eb, Ab and Db. 'Song of Welcome' is in F minor.

'Sandy McNab' is in Ab major.
**Remember**. Two keys that use the same Key Signature are said to be related to each other.
Ab major is the relative major of F minor.
F minor is the relative minor of Ab major.

## Song of Welcome (Israeli)

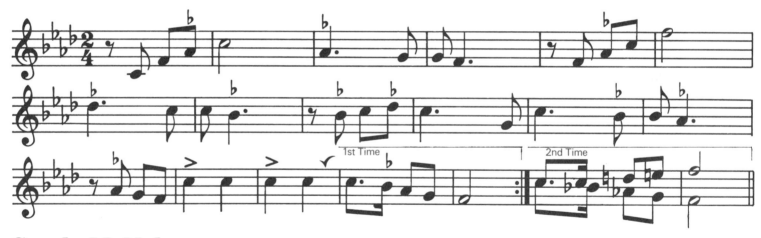

## Sandy McNab (Three-part round)

There was an old fel-low named San-dy Mc-Nab, Who had for his
sup-per a ver-y fine crab, And had to be car-ried home in a cab.

A tune to play **without** D♭ .
'Tum balalyka' is in C minor.
C minor is the relative minor of E♭ major.
E♭ major is the relative major of C minor.
Both keys use three flats: B♭ , E♭ and A♭ .

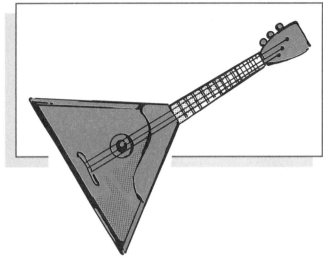

## Tum balalyka (Russian)

## Two new notes at once: C♯ (C sharp) and D♭ (D flat).

Notes lower C sharp and lower D flat both use the same fingering.
Find these notes on the piano chart on page 33.
Both use the same black note.

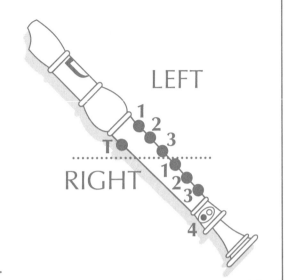

LEFT

1
2
3

T

RIGHT

1
2
3

4

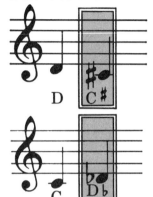

Now play note Lower D.
Carefully add your right fourth finger.
Make sure it only covers the first of the
two small holes.
Use the diagram to help you.
This is the fingering for C♯. Play it.

Now play note Lower C.
Slide your right fourth finger a little to the right.
This uncovers one of the small holes.
This is the fingering for D♭ (same as C♯). Play it.

## Linstead Market (Jamaican folksong)

Car-ry me ac—kee go to Lin-stead Mar-ket, Not a quat-ty would sell.

Car-ry me ac-kee go to Lin-stead Mar-ket, Not a quat-ty would sell. Oh,

Lord! Not a mite not a bite, What a Sat-ur-day night.

Lord! Not a mite not a bite, What a Sat-ur-day night.

# Surabaya Beguine

This tune is in F minor. Take care to play all the flats.

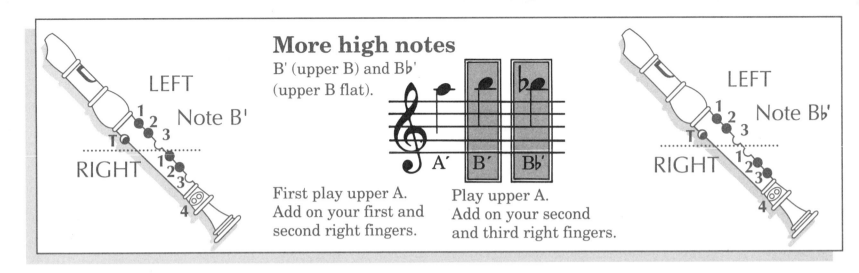

# More high notes

B' (upper B) and Bb' (upper B flat).

First play upper A.
Add on your first and second right fingers.

Play upper A.
Add on your second and third right fingers.

## Minuet (Purcell)

© JCP

## Beckett Blues 1 (12 bar blues)

© JCP

## To play note C" (top C)

First play upper B.
Now take off your left second finger only.
Keep your fingers in position.
This makes top C. Play it.

In the 'Blues' below, remember that A♯' = B♭'.
When you can play "Beckett Blues 2", join it
onto "Beckett Blues 1" to make a longer tune.

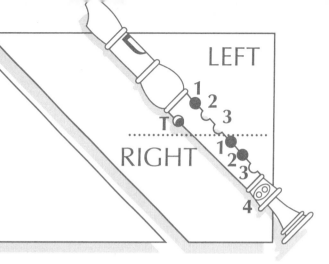

## Beckett Blues 2

© JCP

## Le Basque (French dance)

# Contents

4/95 (1